2015

st Grade

Knights and Castles
and Feudal Life

Walter Buehr brings to life the dramatic era of the feudal castle. Here are the resplendent knights, in training, on their war horses, or going about their day-to-day duties. Here, too, is the rest of the nobility, the peasantry and the clergy, each of them an important part of the feudal system.

Fully illustrated with some of Walter Buehr's most handsome illustrations, this is the perfect book for young people who want to know what it was really like to live in the age of knights and shining armor.

Knight

G. P. Putnam's Sons
New York

and Castles
and Feudal Life

by Walter Buehr

Books by Walter Buehr

Through the Locks: Canals Today and Yesterday
Treasure: The Story of Money and Its Safeguarding
Harbors and Cargoes
Trucks and Trucking
Knights, Castles and Feudal Life
Railroads Today and Yesterday
The Crusaders
Sending the Word: The Story of Communications
The Genie and the Word: Electricity and Communication
Keeping Time
The Story of the Wheel
The World of Marco Polo
The French Explorers in America
The Spanish Armada
The Spanish Conquistadores in North America
Chivalry and the Mailed Knight
Westward — With American Explorers
Heraldry — The Story of Armorial Bearings
Famous Small Boat Voyages
Galleys and Galleons
The Portuguese Explorers
The Viking Explorers
Freight Trains in the Sky

Sixteenth Impression

SBN: GB 399-60341-7

Contents

Feudalism and Life Today

We have all seen pictures of some of the great crumbling castles of medieval Europe. We have seen how their great stone towers and soaring battlements reach high above the humble thatch-roofed villages at their feet. Today these castles lie in silent, ivy-covered ruin and give no hint of lives noble lords and ladies lived behind their massive walls. Their ancient drawbridges have long since crumbled to dust, but once they echoed to the steel-shod hoofs of great war horses, bearing mailed knights.

To understand why, by the thirteenth century, Europe was dotted with strong, thick-walled castles whose owners had to support bands of skilled men-at-arms, we must find out something about medieval society and how it differed from our own. Nowadays we live in an age where the freedom and safety of everybody in the land is taken for granted. If anyone attacks us, steals our goods or money, or trespasses on our property, we can get help. We can go to the nearest policeman, whether we are natives of Oregon, Alabama or Vermont. Today everyone is protected against any aggressor no matter how rich or powerful he may be. Today, disputes are settled in a court of law by a jury made up of fellow citizens, not by some selfish nobleman as they were in feudal days.

Now we are all subject to and protected by the same laws. It would be unthinkable for Chicago to declare war on Milwaukee over a piece of forest land, or for the Mayor of St. Louis to collect tolls from all Mississippi ships carrying freight past his city.

If the owner of some huge ranch in Texas tried to set up his own law courts to sentence his employees to prison terms, he himself would soon be behind bars. What swift punishment would overtake the president of a great steel mill who tried to force his workers to attack a competing mill which was getting too much of his business!

Yet just such things happened every day in medieval Europe and they were accepted as proper.

Probably the greatest point of difference between the thirteenth century and the twentieth is the fact that then the laws were made by the strong and had to be obeyed by the weak, whereas we *elect* the men who make and enforce our laws. They had nothing to say about the laws or those who made them, while we can elect new people whenever we like to change bad governments and bad laws.

During the thirteenth century, Medievalism flourished strongly in England, France, Germany and the rest of western Europe. The word "medieval" means "middle ages." They were the centuries between the "dark ages" — when barbarians overran the Roman Empire, wrecking civilization and reducing Europe to savagery — and the birth of a new day called the Renaissance.

Around the year 700 A.D., Europe was still a continent of darkness. It was peopled with half-savage bands living in crude huts and dressed in skins. Savage clans fought constantly among themselves. In addition to their own battles, the clans were frequently raided by Vikings from Norway.

Reigning over these villages was a King, but even the King dared not move very far from his home. He had little control over his domain; in fact, many of his "subjects" had never even heard of him. The people, on the other hand, got neither help nor protection from the King against Viking raiders or attacks from their own neighbors.

Here and there in England and on the Continent a few stronger and more vigorous leaders tried to protect themselves. They and their followers put up rude forts where the clan could gather with their flocks and herds when attack threatened. Such a fort usually started with a square stone tower of unmortared rocks. This was surrounded by a wooden palisade enclosing a well, a few shelters, and some pens for the livestock. Whenever possible, the fort was built on an island or on top of a steep bank or hill to

9

make defense easier. On the weaker sides of the fort deep ditches were dug and filled with water.

As more of these forts were built the Viking raiders found it harder and harder to sneak up the rivers and surprise the rest of Europe. Finally, after many disastrous attempts, they gave up their raids and were seen no more.

As the countryside grew more settled and the various clans became stronger and more prosperous the chiefs began enlarging and strengthening their small forts. They started to build full-fledged castles which could be defended against anything but a regular siege. Each chief tried to bring more and more of the surrounding villages under his control. He wanted to become so strong that he could demand ennoblement by the King.

The Feudal System

The Nobility

Slowly there emerged in Europe a shaky patchwork kind of authority called fiefdom. In the fiefdom every noble, from the lowliest knight to the most powerful duke, was the vassal of somebody more powerful than he — his suzerain or liege lord. This suzerain or liege lord could demand certain duties and services of his vassals in return for protection against any other more powerful noble.

The King stood at the head of this structure, but he had small control over the dukes and earls who were *his* vassals. They often refused to obey the King's orders and they were powerful enough that they did not have to. The rest of the structure was more rigid. The powerful lords depended upon *their* vassals, nobles of lower rank, for help when they were in trouble. This help they usually received.

A fiefdom was more than just a piece of land with definite boundaries, owned by some nobleman. True enough, it usually contained a castle or smaller fortalice with enough farm land and forest to pay for the upkeep of at least one knight and his war horse. But a fiefdom also included rights. It might include such things as the right to levy tolls for passage over a bridge or along a navigable river, or to fish a certain stretch of a stream, or to operate a mill at which all the peasants had to pay to have their corn ground.

A lord's holdings could be scattered, too. Through inheritance or for other reasons he might hold feudal rights in a fiefdom far from his own, just as he might owe such rights to the lord of some distant castle. A knight or baron seldom owned his lands outright but held them by permission of his suzerain, or overlord, to whom he owed certain feudal duties.

The most important feudal duty was usually that of coming to a liege's aid with all the mailed knights and armed peasant of the fief. This duty usually lasted for a period of forty days and could be required whenever a suzerain called for help to fight an enemy. Sometimes a noblemen owed allegiance to several suzerains because of confusion and overlapping in the feudal system; if any of these should quarrel among themselves, a vassal was really in hot water.

A noble vassal was also expected to help pay for any wars his suzerain waged to defend his fief, for the ransom money to release any of his liege's children held captive by an enemy, for the cost of knighting the suzerain's eldest son, and for the wedding of his eldest daughter. When a suzerain died, his eldest son, providing he had become a worthy knight, would probably be allowed to inherit the fiefdom. He, however, would be taxed a large sum, called a "relief," by his liege lord for the privileges. If the estate went to a more distant relative, the relief was even larger.

Each noble got the money for all these payments by taxing his own lesser vassals, and they, in turn, squeezed it from the commoners and peasants at the bottom of the feudal system. The peasants and commoners paid taxes on everything they raised or manufactured, ate or wore.

The nobility in feudal times was almost entirely hereditary. Unless a man was born into it, he had very little chance of becoming a noble; only rarely was a commoner, because of some special talent or deed, knighted by king or duke.

The nobility, however, had to share some of their special privileges and ownership with another powerful division of feudalism — the Church.

The Cathedral and The Abbey

In the Middle Ages the Church entered the lives of all the people, from king to peasant. Except for a very few Jews, who lived in the market towns, everyone was a devout Catholic. They observed all the Holy Days, kept the Church laws, and paid the heavy Church taxes.

The Church was divided into two great powers. The first of these was the Cathedral. Included in it were the parish priests who, under a bishop, were in charge of the souls of the people. The second power was the Abbey. This included the monasteries, inhabited by different orders of monks under their abbot. They lived a life apart from the everyday world. The monks were the students and learned men of feudal days; in their abbeys were the only libraries of Europe and there the learning — sciences, mathematics, philosophy and medicine — was kept alive during those dark and savage times.

A well-run monastery was a busy place. Unlike the priests, the brothers in an abbey raised and made most of the things they needed as well as caring for the sick and giving to the needy. Much of their time, though, was spent copying manuscripts, the method they used to enlarge their libraries before printing had been invented.

Both the Cathedral and the Abbey were rich and powerful. They had the right to tax the people just as the nobles did, and because the people were close to their Church, they both were constantly receiving rich gifts from those who wanted special favors or to earn forgiveness for some sin. Thus their lands were constantly increasing, to the alarm of the nobles who lost the right to tax a field or a piece of wooded land once it was given to the Church.

Sometimes bishops and abbots kept armed troops of their own and joined with the noble lord in fighting enemies who were as likely to ravage the Cathedral and Abbey as the Castle itself. There were even occasions when the Church forces fought the lord of the manor to settle some bitter dispute.

In contrast to the nobility into which one had to be born, the Church welcomed intelligent commoners. Promising sons of artisans or peasants, as well as the younger sons of

the nobility, were taken in and trained to become priests or monks. The Church, therefore, offered one of the very few chances for a peasant boy to better himself in feudal days; here and there one of them became a bishop or abbot and could meet the nobility on equal terms.

The three great top divisions of feudalism — the nobility, the Church and the Abbey — respected each other and usually got along well, but none of them showed much mercy to the peasants and laborers. It was this class, though, whose taxes paid for the luxurious food, garments, and jewelry and the expensive tournaments of the nobles, as well as the good living, beautiful churches, and altars of the Churchmen.

Classes of Commoners

The commoners, all those who belonged neither to the nobility or to the Church, were divided into several classes. Highest among those living under the banner of the lord of the manor was the bailiff, his agent, who collected taxes and supervised the running of the whole fief. Below the

bailiff in rank were the skilled craftsmen. They planned and carried out everything that was accomplished at the castle and on its lands, since their masters, the nobles, were trained only in the skill of fighting.

Among the craftsmen were the armorers and blacksmiths, the masons and carpenters, the gardeners, stewards, horse-trainers, falconers, game keepers, foresters, weavers and leather-workers. All of these, though they were far beneath the humblest and poorest knight, still enjoyed a much better life than the peasants. The craftsmen were all-important to the well-being of the castle because they provided the skill for everything needed on the estate; only a few things were bought at the fairs or in the market town.

Below the skilled craftsmen were the castle servants — the castle maids and valets, cooks and scullery maids, butlers and pages — who served the family of the lord. They lived within the castle walls and they also had an easier time than did the peasants.

Life Among the Villeins

Now we come to the real underdog of feudalism — the peasant, or villein. In Germany and Middle Europe most of the peasants were serfs, slaves bound permanently to the estates where they were born. By the thirteenth century in England and France, though, he had been freed from serfdom. Here the villein was free to leave his home *if* all his taxes and borrowings were paid up. Few peasants, however, managed to pay their debts, much less save money for a new start. Besides, even if he should decide to leave, there was nowhere to go, since no lord would rent land to a villein who had left his own fief. Actually the feudal villein was not much better off than the serf had been.

He was put on earth, the nobles and churchmen thought, to do all the hard work and serve his betters in every way. There were taxes and charges on everything he did. His bread had to be baked in the lord's ovens, at a charge; his flour ground at the lord's mill, for a fee; his firewood

18

bought from the lord's forester; his grapes pressed in the lord's winepress — with a tax on every gallon.

Not only did the feudal peasant pay a tax on his little farm, but he had to give his lord so many days a month in free labor. He worked on the lord's farms, made repairs on the castle, cleaned the moat, repaired the roads or did any other tasks his sovereign demanded of him. In wartime he had to join his lord's troops. The peasant had to fight his noble master's battles, while the enemy was burning his hut and barns and killing his family.

The villeins lived in miserable huts with mud floors and thatched roofs. There were often no windows in them and usually no chimneys. The fire was built in the middle of the floor and the smoke found its way out through a hole in the roof. There was a bed, in which the whole family

19

slept, a table, and a couple of stools. These, together with a few cooking pots and some wooden plates and spoons, made up the villein's household possessions.

His farm tools might be a spade, a mattock or pickax, a rake and a rude sickle. If the peasant was prosperous, he might even own a wooden plow. His tumble-down shed usually housed a cow, a couple of pigs and a few chickens.

Every member of the villein's family worked in the fields from dawn till dusk. The tiniest children began as soon as they could walk. But with all this work there was still a race with hunger. If a season were too wet or too dry and the crop was small, there was nothing to do by wintertime but beg for bread at the castle gate.

The peasants' clothes were simple, and they used them until they were nothing but rags and the color of earth. The men wore a pair of baggy trousers and a loose blouse — of cloth, leather or sheepskin — held together with a leather belt. Over this, in winter, a thick, woolen home-spun mantle kept out the cold. They wore thick leather shoes, sometimes with wooden soles, which were lined with straw in bitter weather.

The peasant women's garments were primitive too. Occasionally, though, the peasant girls made robes like those worn in the castle and decorated them with embroidery.

On feast days, when the castle called a holiday from work, the villeins had their own games and contests. Wrestling, weight throwing, and cock fighting helped them to forget the miseries of their hard lot. Sometimes they even had a boisterous dance on the green and refreshments that were a gift from the castle.

The Feudal Town

There was one class of commoner which was more or less independent of both the nobles and the Church — those who lived in cities and towns that had obtained Charters of Independence. Although no two charters were exactly alike, they had one similarity — all were contracts freeing the citizens of the town from further feudal duties except that of furnishing armed men if the whole fief were attacked. Such a charter was granted by a suzerain only after payment of a very large relief, or the giving up of some valuable right. After the charter, however, the town could make its own laws, elect its own mayor and aldermen to enforce them, levy its own taxes, and even raise its own army to fend an enemy from the city walls. Only one right was denied to the city or town — the right to coin money; the King alone reserved that privilege.

The feudal town played a very important part in medieval life. Here lived the merchants — commoners, it's true, but often rich and powerful. They imported the goods which noblemen and villeins wanted but were unable to make or raise on the castle lands. To their warehouses came peddlers from the mysterious East, offering richly embroidered cloth and colorful rugs from Persia and India, fragrant herbs and spices from the Eastern Islands, exotic jewelry or keen-bladed swords of Saracen workmanship. Ordinary iron and copper kettles, candlesticks, weapons, and tools also found their way to the merchants' shops.

The town was also the center of manufacturing for medieval Europe. In the thirteenth century there were no factories as we know them, with smoke belching from great chimneys towering above huge, many-windowed buildings. Instead, everything was made by hand in small shops run by a master, three or four helpers, and several apprentices who lived in the upper stories of the building containing the shop.

Each craft was organized into a kind of union, called a guild, whose members specialized in making only one product. A guild, unlike a modern union, had as its members only the master craftsman who owned his own shop; his helpers, called journeymen, and the apprentices had nothing to say in running it. A guild, through its officers, regulated prices, supervised the working conditions and hours, and inspected the quality of the product of the shops belonging to its members.

Each craft was strictly forbidden to make any product of another guild. For instance, a member of the women's shoe guild would be heavily fined if he were caught making a child's shoe or a man's boot.

Guild inspectors also examined the materials and workmanship: a weaver who used shoddy wool in his cloth could expect to be driven out of the guild and have his wares burned publicly.

The guilds guarded their memberships jealously. To become a craftsman, a boy had to be taken as an apprentice into the shop of a master craftsman. He had to sign an agreement, through his parents, to work without pay for seven years while he learned the trade. The master fed and lodged him until the end of his term. Finally the boy was given a suit of clothes and, after passing a guild examina-

tion, the right to seek work as a journeyman under any master.

After a few years as a journeyman a young man could pass another examination and become a master, with the right to open his own shop.

The guilds of the Middle Ages would never allow one master to hire a large number of journeymen. They were afraid he might grow too powerful and thus put others out of business. The whole system in those days was designed to keep shops small.

The first thing that would strike a visitor to a medieval town as he clattered through the gate tower and over the cobbled pavement was the incredible narrowness of the city's streets. They looked like dark, crooked alleys. Houses crowded close on either side; each story overhung the one below it, so that the top floors almost met above the street, allowing little daylight to filter down.

Of course there was no running water, sewers, or street lighting in these medieval towns. Water was drawn from a few wells and all waste and garbage was thrown into the gutter to be taken care of by the street cleaning department — the pigs, dogs and hens. One might think such sanitation methods would mean a lot of sickness and they did. At short intervals great plagues and epidemics swooped down on the town's inhabitants, sometimes taking as much as half the population in one siege.

At night, the inhabitants put up heavy shutters and chained their front doors. Very few people in a feudal town were abroad after dark. Often it was only the watch that could be found, walking the streets with flaming torch and rattle, watching for that most dreaded misfortune —fire. The feudal town, with its wooden, thatched-roofed buildings huddled close together, was a terrible fire hazard. And because the hand bucket brigade was not the most efficient method of fighting flames, many towns were completely wiped out by fire.

During the day the town's streets more than made up for their nighttime loneliness. Each shop front was open to the street, its wares overflowing the pavement. Behind the piles of salable goods were the workrooms where they were made. The owner's family usually lived above the shop; his clerks, porters, and apprentices slept above the family, high up under the eaves.

Usually in a feudal town the shops selling one kind of merchandise were clustered on one street. There was a cheese street, a butcher's alley, a potter's lane with stacks of jugs and dishes, a shoemaker's road, and so forth. When a customer entered a street he was mobbed by clerks and apprentices from all the shops. They pulled at his robe and plucked at his sleeve — each screaming the praises of his shop's wares.

Perhaps life in a feudal, walled town doesn't sound very inviting today. But to the commoners in medieval times it was a whole lot better than being an ever-hungry villein living in a cold, damp mud hut on some lord's estate. There were many villeins, therefore, who despaired of ever getting their debts and taxes paid up and fled to the cities. Once there, if they could hide from the nobleman's bailiff for a year and a day, they were by law out from under the thumb of their suzerain forever.

The Castle

In thirteenth-century Europe a nobleman's castle was much more than a home or a place to entertain his suzerain and his friends. It was a desperate necessity. Without such a stronghold from which he could defend his fief against sudden attack by neighboring barons, his lands and villages were in constant threat of being divided up and distributed among stronger lords.

The suzerain's vassals and the helpless peasants who rented his farms needed this refuge too. They were in particular peril, for an attacker usually killed off the villeins and destroyed the crops and farms of a fief as a quick way to bring surrender.

Several centuries of warfare, sieges, and crusades taught the military engineers of the feudal period how to build a fortress strong enough to resist almost any attack. Many of them had seen a great castle like the Krak de Chevaliers withstand countless attacks. The Krak de Chevaliers was built in the Holy Land as a defense against the Infidels under Saladin.

A well-designed castle was hard to capture. The most effective methods were starving it out — a long job — or taking it by suprise. The designer had to build gates which were difficult to take by a surprise rush, and lay out the walls so that the attacker couldn't get near enough to their bases to raise ladders.

The first step in building a castle was to pick a site with as many natural defenses as possible. Steep, hard-to-climb, rocky cliffs or a rushing stream provided a good natural barrier. Unfortunately, though, many castles had to be built where there were few or even no natural defenses so that the builder had to make up for such lacks by clever design.

Each castle was different because no two sites were alike, but the main plan of defense was the same in all. There was always a tall, very strong tower — round or square — built of fitted stones. Its entrance was usually a small door high off the ground which could be reached only by a wooden stairway that could be knocked down before an attack. This tower was the donjon or keep, where the lord and his men-at-arms could make a last stand if the rest of the castle fell. The keep's small door opened into a great hall with a wide fireplace and often a balcony

across one end of the room. Here the garrison lived and ate. Above were sleeping rooms while at the very top was a gallery so lofty that archers stationed there could overlook and pick off an enemy anywhere on the castle grounds.

The lower part of the donjon was either solid masonry or a vaulted room without stairs to the upper floors. This was used for storage in times of peace.

Many donjons were excavated several levels below ground. The dank, dark cells of the first level were often used as the infirmary or hospital, for medieval doctors thought sunlight was harmful to sick people. The lowest

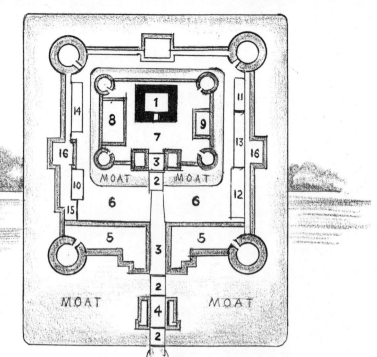

level, its pitch-dark cells dripping with dampness, was reserved for the castle's prisoners. They often spent miserable years there, chained to the cold floor. The word "donjon" thus became "dungeon," meaning an underground prison.

The donjons of the great castles were sometimes over two hundred feet high. They stood in a paved enclosure called the "inner bailey," and they were always well stocked with provisions in the event of a siege.

The wooden or stone palace where the lord and his family lived also stood in the inner bailey. It had large windows, decorative carvings, and many small turrets and

29

chimneys. Here the family slept and dined, played games and sewed, entertained their friends and held the great banquets feudal nobility loved so well.

The castle chapel was also to be found in the inner bailey. Religion was such an important part of feudal life that most castles kept a chaplain to hold private services for family and retainers.

The inner bailey was enclosed by a high wall of stone. This was topped by a broad walk protected on the outer side by a stone parapet. These "curtain" walls were from six to fifteen feet thick and from twenty to thirty feet high. Towers were built out from the corners of the wall and at intervals along it; a larger tower stood at each side of the entrance gate.

The towers were important for defense of the wall. Archers, stationed at slit windows, could shoot attackers at the base of the curtain wall. If the enemy managed to scale the parapet, the doors to the towers on each end of the captured section were barred, thus penning up the besiegers.

During a siege wooden platforms, called hoards or brattices, were built four or five feet out from the parapets. These had slits in their floors so the defenders could pour stones, boiling oil, or pitch on the heads of any enemy digging below at the base of the walls. The hoards had roofs and wooden sides to shelter the archers. These were covered with wet cow hides to keep them from catching fire when hit by flaming arrows or Greek fire — a chemical mixture which burned fiercely.

The weakest point of the castle, the entrance gate, was

carefully designed to allow as many different defenses as possible. The entire gateway was surrounded by a lower wall, called the barbican. This had another gate of its own to keep the enemy from rushing the main gate before it could be closed. Once inside the barbican a broad ditch or moat, sometimes filled with water, barred the way to the main gate.

The moat was spanned by a hinged bridge which could be raised in the event of attack. Behind the drawbridge was a pair of massive oak doors faced with iron plates. These were barred with heavy beams.

An enemy that managed to get through all these obstacles found even more defenses awaiting him. The entrance to the castle itself was usually a long tunnel without doors or windows. High up along the sides of the wall were arrow slits and in the ceiling there were holes, called machiolations, through which boiling water, melted lead, or hot oil could be poured on the foe.

The other end of the tunnel was barred by a portcullis, a grilled gate which could be raised. With the portcullis down, the foe found himself trapped in the tunnel with no way of escape.

If the besiegers got past all the outer defenses and into the *outer* bailey, they were confronted by the moat, drawbridge, and curtain walls of the *inner* bailey. This was a complete fort, a smaller scale of the one they had just stormed.

Some castles had as many as three or four rings of walls. This meant that if the enemy reached a wall to overrun a bailey inside, he could be attacked from the walls in front

of him as well as from the wall towers behind him. Each tower was a separate unit that could go on fighting on its own.

The outer bailey, which contained huts sheltering workmen, livestock, and food, was stripped clean by the defenders before the enemy appeared. When the supplies were safe inside the inner bailey, all the huts were burned to keep them out of the attackers' hands.

Beyond the outer walls of the castle lay open country. There was not a building, a tree, or even a bush within a quarter of a mile of the great towering building — nothing but bare ground or sparse grass. There was no cover to shelter an enemy trying to rush the gate.

The lack of trees around the medieval castle provided still another protection to its dwellers. There was no timber with which the attacker could build fires in his effort to burn the main oak gate.

The Siege

Feudal Siege Weapons

You might think that one look at the strong medieval castle — its moats, high walls and grim towers, its defenses within defenses — would discourage any enemy from attempting a siege. This, however, was not the case. Even the strongest castles were stormed and taken, in a time when cannon and gunpowder were still unknown.

Even without gunpowder, feudal engineers managed to invent very destructive weapons. The smallest was the bow — either the English longbow or the crossbow — used by the lightly armored infantry. The crossbow, favored in France and Germany, had a wooden stock shaped like a rifle. A very stiff steel bow was attached across the front. Because it was too stiff to bend by hand, this bow was sprung with the help of a small windlass which pulled the bowstring back over a notched trigger. When the trigger was released, the string sent a heavy bolt, as the short arrow was called, a great distance with terrific force. A bolt from a heavy arbalest could go through a coat of mail at 375 yards and it had a range of over 1,400 feet.

The English yew bow, much lighter than the arbalest, was about six feet long. It looked much like the modern target bow and had a range of about 220 yards. The long-bow, handled by a good English archer, was extremely accurate. And it could shoot five times as fast as the cross-bow.

There were many types of engines to hurl great stones, heavy arrows, and fire bombs. Some were enormous cross-bows; others were like huge slingshots. Still others got their power from a heavy beam which was sprung back with twisted ropes. When this was released suddenly against the missile, it was like a baseball bat hitting a home run.

There were also stone throwers with beams that were operated by heavy counterweights. These engines had odd and wonderful names such as Petriaria, Ballista, Mangonal, Catapult, and Scorpion and were used to batter down walls and towers. They were also used to hurl casks of Greek fire — a mixture of pitch, naptha, and sulphur — into the bailey to set fire to anything burnable.

To smash gates or weak walls, a "cat" was used. This was a huge battering ram hung by chains on a heavy wheeled frame. This could be moved up and swung against a gate until it gave way. The cat had a roof of hide-covered beams to protect the men operating it against the stones and hot pitch poured from the walls above.

To cross a deep moat, men carried thousands of bundles of brush and sticks and tossed them into the moat until it was filled. The men who carried these fagots or bundles were protected by a covered passageway. This was made of timbers covered with hides and was called a penthouse. Using it, they could drag their loads to the moat in safety.

If the walls of the enemy's castle were built on rock too solid to tunnel under, or if they were too thick to batter down and too high to climb with ladders, there was only one solution — to build the biggest and most spectacular

of all siege engines, the siege tower. This was a very tall, movable tower of heavy wooden beams, its front sheathed and covered with wet hides. On top of the tower was a shielded platform which could be reached by ladders. The drawbridge attached to it could be lowered to the castle walls.

After the moat had been filled, the siege tower was trundled over the causeway on rollers, under cover of a hail of bolts and stones from the catapults behind them. When the siege tower was near enough, the drawbridge was dropped on the parapet. Then a wave of howling bowmen, knights, and men-at-arms, with naked blades flashing and battle-axes whirling, leaped down upon the defenders manning the walls. They were followed by re-inforcements who swarmed up the siege tower's ladders.

A Typical Siege

To watch a typical siege, let us follow the course of an attack on an imaginary castle, somewhere in England around the year 1150 A.D. Several days ago the enemy lord, Viscount Chester, had sent a young squire to fling down the gauntlet before the Baron Adelbert. By tossing the glove on the floor before the Baron, Lord Chester had declared war — war over an unsettled dispute about the ownership of two villages each lord claimed.

A few hours ago scouts had reported the approach of an invader, and Baron Adelbert, lord of Castle Flintrock, and all of his men-at-arms were on the alert. The last of the terrified villeins had hustled his wife, children, and the family pig over the drawbridge spanning the green-scummed moat. Slowly the drawbridge was drawn back and behind it, the great gates clanged shut. The massive bolts were pulled into place.

Along the high parapets, workmen nailed wet hides to the wooden hoards hanging out over the walls; others lugged great piles of stones for ammunition to the towers and battlements. Firewood, too, was carried up to heat the caldrons of water and pitch that were to repel anyone who attempted to climb the scaling ladders. Crossbowmen cranked up their bows and filled leather bags with heavy bolts, the arrows of war. At last Baron Adelbert and his Seneschal, second in command, agreed that they were ready.

Far down the road which led to Cairnloch Castle sunlight flashed on naked steel. Behind the far-off trees a body of horsemen appeared, glittering in their armor, bright-

colored shields, and shining lances tipped with fluttering
pennons. The horsemen were followed by a long column
of steel-helmeted men-at-arms bearing long pikes and
bright battle-axes. Bringing up the rear was a scattered
mob of villeins armed with their scythes, pruning hooks,
and homemade spears. With them was a procession of

carts and wagons carrying tents, food, and all the supplies necessary to carry on the siege.

Just outside the range of the castle's arbalests, or cross-

bowmen, Lord Chester's men halted. A herald stepped forth and in a loud voice demanded the castle's surrender.

When this invitation was declined with jeers, the war was on. The invaders unsaddled. They posted sentries, set up their tents, and built their cooking fires. Meanwhile Lord Chester, his knights, and a hired siege engineer held a council of war.

This engineer, although he was only a villein, was famous for directing successful sieges. The Viscount had to pay him a large fee in gold in order to persuade him to take on the job. Although the feudal knights were good in man-to-man open combat, when skill and planning were needed they often had to turn to some commoner.

By the next morning every peasant within miles who hadn't fled to the castle was driven into the forest to help cut timber. They were to build a palisade encircling the whole castle and thus prevent aid from Baron Adelbert's relatives or allies. Humbert, the siege engineer, began assembling his siege engines and building new ones.

The siege engineer had several plans of attack open to him. He could decide to starve out the garrison, but that would be very slow. Humbert decided against this plan because of the risk that Viscount Chester's allies would get tired of sitting and go home or that his own vassals, who were only obliged to give him forty days' service, might be free to leave before the siege was over.

Humbert decided upon a twofold attack. Work was begun on a tall siege tower in full view of the enemy. But at the same time workers started digging a tunnel under cover of a large penthouse. It was aimed straight at one of

42

the corner towers. Day after day the siege tower grew taller and the workers drove their tunnel closer to the tower.

When the workers were directly under the tower, they began enlarging the hole beneath the foundations, carefully bracing with heavy timbers. They finished just as the last spike was hammered into the tower. The attack was ready!

Pushed from behind by hundreds of villeins, the great siege tower moved over the wooden rollers set ahead of it. It was rolled across the filled-in moat until it stood only a dozen feet from the castle walls. The battlements opposite it were crowded with a solid mass of mailed knights, pikemen, arbalests — almost the entire garrison. They stood ready to offer combat when the drawbridge dropped.

But all was quiet on the tower. As minutes without action passed, an uneasy murmur rose from the defenders. Why didn't they attack; was this some trick? Suddenly a panic-stricken shriek rose from the sentry on the other side of the castle. "Smoke," he yelled. "Smoke coming from under the north tower!" The Baron knew only too well what that meant, but it was too late. He had been tricked into believing the attack was coming from the siege tower and had forgotten to have sentries listen for the sound of digging.

Had Baron Adelbert known, he could have started a counter-tunnel and broken into Humbert's before it reached the tower. But now the timbers holding up the foundations of the tower were afire; when they burned through it would collapse. Before anyone had time to

think, a sharp crack resounded through the smoky air and the whole north tower crumbled to the ground.

The Viscount's waiting troops surged through the breach, completely undefended because all the castle garrison faced the siege tower. The attackers spread through the grounds, driving before them the few men they met. Then as the harried garrison turned from the siege tower to meet the new threat, the drawbridge suddenly dropped and a wave of attackers fell upon them from behind. The Baron's men were trapped, and after a few minutes of hopeless combat, the garrison surrendered. The proud banner of Flintrock Castle fluttered down the staff and Lord Chester's triumphant pennon took its place. The siege was over.

The Mailed Knight

A Knight's Training

We have seen how the medieval castle was the center of feudal life, the well-being of the whole fief depending upon it. It was the strongest defense against any invader, and its noble lord and his knights formed the heart of its fighting force.

The great difference between men of noble blood and all commoners was skill in armed combat. From early childhood the young noble was trained in handling arms and taught that fighting was the greatest art. While the young son of the villein labored in the fields with scythe and hoe the baron's young son practiced fencing, riding, and tilting.

46

A twelfth- or thirteenth-century knight, mounted on his great war horse, encased in chain mail and flourishing his long two-edged sword, could easily rout eight or ten bareheaded villeins armed only with pikes or clubs. In feudal times the mounted knight was the backbone of the army. The foot soldiers were looked on with contempt and were expected to retreat in panic before the charge of knightly cavalry.

Now let's find out how a boy of noble blood became a knight and how he learned to use the tools of his warlike trade. Knighthood was a noble estate and had to be worked for and deserved before it was granted; noble birth did not automatically entitle a youth to it.

By the time the son of a noble was ten he was having riding lessons, practicing tilting, learning swordsmanship and the use of the light crossbow. When he reached his teens he was sent to a castle as a squire, or apprentice, to learn the skills and traditions a knight must know. It was customary for each lord of a castle to take into his own household the sons of several of his noble allies or relatives. It was felt that a boy would have a better chance under the eye of someone other than his own father.

As a squire the boy learned how to take care of his master's lance, sword, and armor, as well as his great war horse. He and the other squires held mock tournaments where they tried to unhorse each other with light lances. They practiced their swordsmanship against each other. They sat for long hours at the feet of some grizzled knightly teacher who told them of their duties and responsibilities.

When at last the noble lord felt that his pupil was worthy, an adubment was held. Beginning with night-long vigil and solemnities in the church, this was followed by a great celebration in the castle. The climax came as the young man received the knightly buffet, a mighty blow on the head by the clenched fist of his sponsor. The sponsor then raised him from the floor, kissed him on both cheeks, and dubbed him knight.

Soon the newly dubbed knight was surrounded by noble relatives. They pressed about him with congratulations, presented him with a suit of bright, shining armor, a new sword, and a lance. They gave him a shield decorated with his new coat of arms, and a strong sleek war horse of his own. Now he could take his place alongside the other noble knights of chivalry.

If a young knight was lucky enough to be born to a family rich in lands and estates he might be given a small fortalice with farms and forest. Or, if he were an oldest son, he eventually would inherit his father's lands and castle. However, many a knight of poor family, or a younger

son who couldn't inherit the family lands, remained land-less all his life. It was his lot to hire out as the paid retainer of some richer noble.

Knightly Armor and Arms

Fighting men began wearing body armor far back in history. The earliest armor was simply a heavy leather jacket or padded coat. Then overlapping scales of iron or bronze were sewn to the leather jacket to add more pro-tection. By the twelfth century, however, almost all armor was chain mail, a type the Crusaders had seen the Saracens use in the Holy Land.

A hooded mail shirt or hauberk, covering the body, arms, and legs to the shins, was a garment no one but a noble could hope to own. Such a shirt was made up of as many as 250,000 separate handmade and hand-tempered steel rings. These were interlaced and each one was sep-arately riveted. It took an expert armorer three years to make such a shirt for he could do only about 250 rings a day. A glittering coat of mail like this would cost a knight about $12,000, at today's values.

Over the mail hood the knight wore a plain conical steel

cap or a helmet which covered his entire head. The knight's helmet rested on his shoulders and was held in place by straps buckled to the hauberk. Although helmets gave extra protection, it was difficult for the knight to see out of the eye slits. He also found the headgear heavy and clumsy. For this reason he usually wore his helmet only at the start of actual combat. Later on better helmets were developed. These had face openings and hinged visors which could be pulled down over the face before the battle.

A coat of chain mail weighed 20 to 30 pounds and could turn the thrust of any lance or sword. When it was worn over a heavily padded jacket it could usually resist the blow of a club or battle-axe.

The quality of a suit of armor was described as "proof." "Full proof" meant it was able to withstand the bolt from a heavy crossbow, while "half-proof" meant it was good against an arrow from a light crossbow or a longbow.

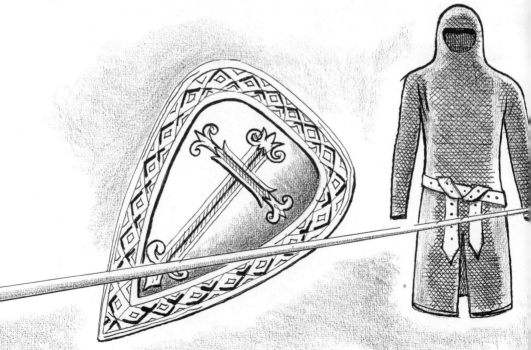

Tilting armor, used in tournaments where knights rode against each other with leveled lances, was one of the heaviest suits of armor. Sometimes it weighed as much as 125 pounds, with its huge helmet weighing nearly 40 pounds. Wearing it, a knight had to be lifted into the deep saddle on his war horse. His armor was so heavy that he could not mount unaided nor get up off the ground if felled. And a knight's armor was not all his equipment. He also carried a shield of thick hide stretched over a wooden frame. This he held in front of him by thrusting his left arm through two handles. The shield was curved, both to protect his body more fully and to provide an angle so that the enemy's lance would glance off it more easily. Upon the shield was blazoned the knight's coat-of-arms.

The mounted knight carried several weapons. First was the wooden, steel-tipped lance, which he carried under his right armpit while attacking. In addition to this he had a long two-edged sword, a short sword, and perhaps a mace — a club with a round spiked tip.

A fully armored knight, with sinister helmet and great shield, thundering along on a huge armored war horse, must have struck terror to the poor villein with only a sharpened stick for a weapon. The knight was indeed the Sherman tank of the thirteenth century.

But there *was* one great weakness. Armor became so heavy that if the knight was unhorsed he had to lie as help-less as a turtle on its back until somebody lifted him up. It is easy to imagine how he must have felt on a hot summer day, encased in padded leather clothes and a hundred or more pounds of sizzling iron.

A Battle Between Nations

Feudal Europe lived under an uneasy peace constantly broken by small baronial feuds. Often these were between two petty nobles, their vassals, and allies, with the armies consisting of only a couple of hundred knights and men-at-arms and a mob of half-armed villeins. During these campaigns few of the knights were hurt but often great numbers of peasants were killed. Their huts were burned and their crops trampled so that the lord of the castle might lose part of his tax income.

These small feuds were bad enough, but occasionally warfare between two nations broke out, with as many as 50,000 men joining in battle. At such a time the King sent out a call to all his vassals for aid. As this was their feudal

53

duty every vassal set about collecting his army. There was
a great bustling and uproar in every castle of the land.

The royal dukes mustered their own knights and men-
at-arms and called out *their* vassals to do the same. Every
able-bodied peasant was conscripted and handed a pike or
axe; all carts, horses, and mules were commandeered to

carry supplies. Even the free walled towns had to furnish an army of their own citizens, under command of the mayor or a councilman. People from everywhere marched to battle, all moving to the rallying place where the King's banner had been planted.

A great medieval battle was a colorful sight. Arrayed across the field were the close-packed companies of villeins, flanked by archers in shining steel caps and breastplates. Behind them, ready to go into action when the

villeins had retreated, stood a long row of mounted knights. They looked splendid, plumes waving, helmets glittering, brilliantly emblazoned surcoats and bright chain-mail hauberks shining in the sun. Their huge snorting chargers tossed armored heads and pawed the ground. Behind each knight rode his squire, holding aloft on his lance tip the bright-colored, fluttering banner of his liege; and behind him the mounted sergeants and men-at-arms awaited battle.

As the enemy charged, clouds of arrows rose from the ranks of bowmen, many to find their mark. But the line thundered ahead, reaching the first group of villeins. The long swords of the knights caused fearful damage to the fleeing peasants, who with the archers took refuge behind the lines of their own knights.

Now the real clash occurred as armor met armor in desperate hand-to-hand battle on horseback. It was here that the engagement was decided. In spite of the fierceness of the combat, though, surprisingly few of the armored knights were killed. Although there were battered heads and bloody wounds aplenty, it was always among the villeins that the losses ran highest.

The battle raged but at last one side began to retire, still fighting stubbornly. Soon the whole line was in headlong flight, leaving the victors to do what they would to the straggling foot soldiers. When all was over, the King thanked all his loyal vassals, gave them a great banquet, and sent each lord back to his own castle. All that was left of the colorful battle was the troubadors' victory song.

Daily Life of the Castle

A Visit To A Feudal Castle

Let us pay a peacetime visit to a feudal lord's castle to see what it looked like when there was no threat of war. As we approach the grim, walled fortress we can see that the drawbridge is down and the gates stand open. Merchants and villeins cluster before the porter, stating their business and awaiting permission to enter.

Visitors of high rank, equal to or greater than the lord, were greeted at the gate by the lord himself. He himself led their horses into the courtyard, helped them to dismount, and gave them a kiss of greeting. Lesser visitors were met by the lord's first squire.

Everyone was welcome at a feudal castle; the household

57

was so starved for news of the outside world that any passing traveler was expected to stay for several days at least. He was feasted and wined and asked to tell all the gossip he knew. Jongleurs especially were welcomed. They were the wandering minstrels and jugglers, who could sing a song, tell a story, and do a few magic tricks. They made it their business to be full of the news of the whole countryside. But castle hospitality extended to everyone. Even the lowliest villein, on an errand for his liege, was always sure of a good meal and a bed on the rushes of the floor.

As we approach the castle gate, we are waved in by the porter. We cross the drawbridge and enter the dark tunnel of the main gate, to emerge into the busy confusion of the outer bailey. Pigs and hens compete for choice bits of trash, while ducks waddle around the muddy puddles in the cobbled courtyard. A great clanging and a shower of sparks from the door of a shed indicates the smithy, where armorers are repairing armor and forging weapons. Ear-splitting screams and shrieks issue from the mews where the hawker is feeding the coursing birds. Peasants' carts loaded with cabbage and turnips creak toward the storehouses, and villeins emerge from the bakehouse with baskets of fresh-baked loaves.

We leave the tumult of the outer bailey and pass through the great gate into the inner bailey. Here everything is quieter and much cleaner: no piles of trash are stacked against the walls of thatched huts, and pigs, fowls and curs are kept out. Before us lies the great keep, silent and unoccupied now, and to the left is the handsome palace, which is the home of the lord and his family — the hub of castle life. Pages, maids, and villein servants bustle in and out on castle errands, and occasionally a noble comes out, dressed in silks and fur. He mounts a horse that is brought to the door and clatters through the gate, scattering the commoners in his path.

The main room of the palace is the great hall, with its lofty timbered ceiling and dark, paneled walls. The walls are solid except where they are pierced by tall windows filled with real glass. The windowpanes are tiny and set in heavy lead frames. Several of the windows have beautiful red-, blue-, and yellow-colored glass which makes the room glow. Rich rugs and tapestries hang upon the walls, above heavily carved oaken chests.

Opposite the fireplace, big enough to hold several enormous logs, is a raised dais or platform, on which stand several massive canopied chairs. Here the master, his family and especially honored guests will sit at meals or other gatherings. Long oaken tables stretch across the room, flanked by low benches, where the lower ranks sit at meals. At mealtimes the tables are always crowded because the castle feeds a great many mouths.

Feudal Furnishing and Clothing

The medieval great hall was a mixture of luxury and extreme discomfort. It was filled with beautiful carving, stained-glass windows and rare tapestries, but the floors were of stone, covered by a thick layer of rushes cut in the swamps. The rushes served the double purpose of keeping the feet warm and hiding the bones and scraps thrown to the dogs at meals. When the rush "carpet" got too dirty, the servants simply spread another layer of clean rushes on top. The tapestries, too, were useful as well as ornamental; they helped shut off the icy drafts from the cracks in the walls.

The lord of the castle got up at 4:30 or 5:00 in the morning and bathed in a large tub of hot water brought in by a couple of husky villeins. Although there was no plumbing of any kind in a medieval castle, the nobility bathed often and changed clothes frequently. There was no shortage of servants, because any village boy or girl would have jumped at the chance to work at the palace in exchange for meals and a suit of clothes. There were even plenty of laundresses to do the huge castle wash. They washed by the method still used today in many parts of Europe. They laid the wet soapy garments on a flat stone and beat them with another. The question of money wages for any of these services never occurred to either master or servant.

The noblemen of this period were smooth-shaven and trimmed their hair in a fairly long bob. The villein, however, never saw a razor; his beard and hair was likely to be a matted jungle.

Though people of gentle blood kept themselves clean, this was about as far as feudal sanitation went. Medieval doctors were good at bleeding their patients for any ailment and at prescribing mysterious powders made of dried bats' blood, powdered pearls, or fingernail parings. But they had never heard of germs or infection. People drank from the same streams in which they washed clothes and dumped refuse. In the kitchen, rats, flies and roaches were taken for granted.

Rooms in feudal castles were large but few in number, so that the lady of the palace thought nothing of asking several guests to share the master bedroom. The bedroom of the lord and lady usually had one enormous canopied bed, piled high with feather quilts and fitted with heavy curtains. These were always drawn shut before going to

sleep. Medieval people believed that night air was poisonous and they tried hard to keep it out of the bedroom. A few hard chairs and several chests with hinged lids completed the bedroom furniture. Several wall tapestries and a couple of fur rugs and of course the usual fireplace relieved the bareness.

By the thirteenth century, people had pretty well given up wearing garments which had to be wrapped around them and then tied, in the Roman style. Their clothes were now cut to fit, with sleeves and necks, and had to be pulled on. Mostly they were made of wool clipped from the backs of the manorial sheep and spun, woven and sewed by the castle servingwomen. However, more and more linen was spun from home-grown flax, and peddlers were beginning to bring in beautiful silk and cotton fabrics from the East. These finer fabrics were worn mainly by members of the nobility.

The typical lord at a castle was dressed for the day by one of his many valets. His underclothes were made of fine white linen. Next he put on a pair of wool or silk stockings dyed some somber color. Then came an open-necked shirt of white linen, and over this a long robe, often fur-trimmed. His outermost garment, a tunic, was pulled on over his head and usually belted at the waist. Shoes were either of leather or cloth, sometimes embroidered and set with jewels. For outdoor wear the lord had a wide cloak, often fur-lined and trimmed. Fur was worn only by those of noble blood; penniless knights wore their ragged but fur-trimmed cloaks even in hot weather to proclaim to all their gentle birth.

The garments of the lady of the palace were much like her husband's but were made of finer stuff. There were shimmering silks, wool and cotton in rich patterns, heavy gold embroidery. Women wore chamois-skin gloves and pointed shoes of velvet or silk. These were embroidered and jewel-encrusted and tied with colored silk ties. Some of the lady's outer robes were close-fitting with long, trailing sleeves. These were held in place by girdles richly decorated and set with precious stones.

Household Tasks

The palace household awaked early and by five in the morning everyone was astir. Breakfast came early too, but it was skimpy — only a piece of bread and a glass of thin wine. By mid-morning everybody was hungry so that dinner was served around ten in the morning, with supper around five.

Everyone went to bed shortly after dark unless some celebration or entertainment by the jongleurs kept them up late. With only smoky torches and dim candles to light the great, high-ceilinged rooms the castle was a dark and shadowy place after dark. And with only fireplaces to combat drafts from the icy walls and stone floors, it was a cold place, too. It was not surprising that householders found an early bedtime the best way to escape these nighttime discomforts.

The lord of the manor had plenty of activities with which to fill his day. After attending Mass in the chapel and breakfasting, he listened to reports from his steward. Then he inspected the falcon house and the stables. Later, he settled the bailiff's complaints about the peasants and ordered punishment for thieves and poachers among the villeins.

His lady meanwhile was busy with the running of the vast castle household. With her huge key ring swinging on its silver chain, she walked along the castle corridors. She unlocked closets, cupboards, and chests. Carefully she doled out to the cooks and maids the daily allotment of food and other supplies. Then she looked in on the many apartments to see that they were properly cleaned.

The mistress of the castle was in charge of the clothes-making industry of the fief. She supervised the group of maids who spun the thread and wove it into cloth; who cut and sewed the cloth into garments for every man, woman and child in the castle.

The lady also took care of the training of all girl children of the family. And she trained all boys, too — until they were old enough to begin preparing for knighthood.

Feudal Games and Sports

Although castle life was busy there was plenty of time for play too. On days when the weather was bad, the noble families loved all sorts of parlor games, some of them very much like our own. They also played board games such as checkers and backgammon. But what a nobleman loved best was outdoor sport, especially on horseback, and here he excelled.

To enter the lists at a tournament and unseat your opponent was to the nobleman the greatest of sporting pleasures. Next best was to hunt with spears the fierce wild boar

and the savage bear of the forest. Or to chase the red deer and bring it down with a bolt from the crossbow.

Game was not hard to find in feudal Europe, for great forests covered most of the countryside. Bears and wolves, made bold by hunger, had been known to attack people in the very streets of the towns.

All game was reserved for the nobility. The noble had a right to hunt and fish whenever and wherever he pleased, but no villein dared kill a wild animal or take a fish from a stream. The peasants were not even permitted to shoot the deer or wild boars that were uprooting their crops. If they

trapped a hare it was called poaching and for this crime a
villein risked a death sentence.

In feudal days both lords and ladies were skilled at fal-
conry. This sport, very popular then, is so rare today that
few people know what it is.

The falconer, or hawker, got his birds by climbing a tall
tree and robbing the hawk's nest of its fledglings. Then
came a long period of training the young birds to hunt.
After patient teaching, the young hawk learned to sit
quietly upon the gloved wrist of his trainer, wearing a
hood which covered his head. When the hawker spied a
heron or duck flying high overhead, he slipped off the
hood and threw his falcon into the air. In a flash, the
speedy hunting hawk went after his victim. He pounced
with razor-sharp talons and brought the limp and dangling
bird back to his master. A good falcon or hunting hawk
was prized almost as highly as a war horse and made a
fine gift for a king or great noble.

A feudal hunting party must have been a fine sight indeed. The huntsmen wore bright costumes, and each carried a tall hooded hawk on his gauntleted wrist. Mounted on their dapple-gray palfreys, they crashed over fences, leaped brooks and thundered across fields of grain. This was great pleasure to the huntsmen but to the peasant whose crops were being trampled it was a tragedy. It spelled hunger or even starvation to his family, but he dared not utter a complaint.

Feudal Dining

The noble folk of feudal castles were prodigious meat-eaters and sat down to many dishes which would seem

strange to us now. Swans, peacocks, thrushes, blackbirds, storks, and cuckoos all went into the oven for special feasts. So did all manner of game — rabbits, venison, bear, and wild boar. The nobles preferred game to butcher's meat, but they did eat huge quantities of beef, veal, lamb, and pork. They were particularly fond of pork and the pig was the ever-present animal in the feudal scene.

Fresh-water fish, eels, frogs, and snails were enjoyed, especially on Holy Days when meat was forbidden. There were even times when salt fish, carted from the coast, could be had. Vegetables were used sparingly — generally as flavoring for meat dishes — but fruits, fresh, stewed or cooked in wine, were great favorites.

There were no iceboxes or canned foods in feudal kitchens so all fresh meat had to be eaten at once or salted. Salting was the only way medieval cooks had to preserve meat. Because fresh meat spoiled in a very short time, especially in warm weather, medieval cooks disguised the taste of their meat dishes with all manner of herbs and spices. They used cloves, mace, saffron, ginger, and cinnamon liberally, even though spices came from the faraway East and were very expensive.

The gap between what the nobles ate and the villeins' coarse fare was enormous. The peasants seldom tasted meat, their only chance being when a feast day at the castle brought them the scraps or when a peasant dared to poach a rabbit from the lord's garden. From day to day they lived on coarse black bread, and soup made from the vegetables in their gardens. Medieval gardens grew most of the vegetables we know today.

A Feudal Tourney

Life in a medieval castle was likely to grow dull and humdrum during times of peace. Castles were too far apart for casual visiting. The wretched roads and the danger of attack by bandits made travelers few and far between.

To break the monotony of castle life, any excuse was reason enough to hold a tournament. It might be the adubment of a son, the marriage of a daughter, or a visit by suzerain or bishop. Then a tournament was held to which all the nobility within riding distance were invited. Everyone in the fief looked forward joyfully to the excitement of a three-day tournament.

A great banquet was always given on the eve of the tourney. By three o'clock the guests sat down to dinner, the higher nobles in the castle's great hall, the lower ranks at tables set up outside the walls near the lists. Each place at table was set with a spoon and a knife (forks had not yet been invented). There was also a drinking goblet, silver for the higher nobles, wood or leather for lesser ones. The important guests ate from silver plates but everyone else used a thick slice of bread, called a trencher, on which his meat was placed. When the meal was finished, the trenchers and other uneaten scraps were gathered in baskets and given to the poor. The bones were tossed to the dogs that lay in wait under the tables, and the company settled back to watch the antics of a company of jongleurs. They applauded a minstrel who sang a song complimenting the host and hostess and the higher guests. At last the shadows lengthened and the host called for a final cup of wine.

Dawn had scarcely come to the eastern sky when the brazen-voiced trumpets pealed out the opening of the tourney. The nobles and their ladies quickly took their places in the pennon-trimmed pavilions. Next richly-attired heralds appeared at the end of the lists, flourishing long golden trumpets. They led the procession of mounted mailed knights, two by two, past the cheering stands.

Jousting in feudal times was more than a mere sport. It was the place where a young knight learned his business. All knights agreed that jousting, which was frowned on by the Church and often resulted in death or serious injury, was absolutely necessary to train young knights. In the lists he got his first taste of what he must face later in battle.

During a friendly tourney, two knights dressed in full armor and mounted on great war horses faced each other from opposite ends of the lists. Each crouched behind his shield, and clutched firmly in his right hand a long wooden lance with a blunted tip. At the signal they plunged toward each other at full gallop, each aiming his lance tip at the other. The object was to strike the opponent's shield hard enough to splinter the lance, and if possible to knock him out of the saddle.

If three lances were broken by each knight, a draw was called and another pair of jousters took the field. If, however, a knight was unhorsed or lost his lance, he had to pay the winner a ransom or forfeit his horse and armor.

The jousting, feasting, and other tourney entertainment usually lasted for three days. Finally the excitement dwindled, the guests went home, and the castle resumed its placid way of life.

Index